# Elgar Country

by

## Barry Collett

illustrated by

## Pauline Collett

*For Robert,*
*With all good wishes.*

*Barry Collett*

*Pauline Collett.*

Thames Publishing
14 Barlby Road, London, W10 6AR

*May 2001.*

*Printed by John G Eccles Printers Ltd, Inverness*

# Contents

# Acknowledgements

I wish to register my thanks to the following people for their help in the compiling of this book: Alan Webb and Jack McKenzie, former Curators of the Elgar Birthplace Museum; Raymond Monk for his kind permission to use the photographs in the book, and the quotation from Carice Elgar Blake's Elgar Ledger Notes; to Ken and Marion Simmons for accompanying us on many happy visits and quests around Elgar Country, and for information from their own invaluable research now published by the Elgar Society as *The Elgars of Worcester';* to Novello and Company Ltd for permission to use the musical quotations; to my friend and publisher John Bishop for his patience and encouragement; and finally to my wife Pauline for her help in countless ways, and whose own researches have led to two further Elgar books.

B. C.
May 1986

# Illustrations

To
Ludlow

Leominster

Bromyard

Witley
Court

R. Teme

Broadheath

A44

Claines

To
Droitwich

WORCESTER

A44

Spetchley

A422

To
Stratford-
upon-Avon

Powick

Storridge

A4103

Madresfield

Great
Malvern

Kempsey

Croome
Court

Drakes
Broughton

Pershore

R. Lugg

A465

Worcestershire
Beacon

To
Evesham

R. Wye

HEREFORD

A49

Mordiford

Ledbury

A4103

Malvern Hills

Malvern Wells

Little Malvern

Herefordshire
Beacon

A38

Longdon

Tewkesbury

R. Severn

A449

Radmarley
d'Abitot

Ross on Wye

Hasfield
Court

To
Cheltenham

A40

GLOUCESTER

Monmouth

0 1 2 3 4 5 Miles

**7**

# Introduction

Elgar country—that most beautiful stretch of West Country England bounded by the three cathedral cities of Worcester, Hereford and Gloucester. It is a landscape of rolling, wooded hills; of quiet leafy lanes and small, black-and-white timbered villages; of apple orchards and the majestic Rivers Severn and Wye; and more or less at the centre, rising steeply from the plain, the long sweep of the Malvern Hills, with their ceaselessly changing coloured hues reflecting the play of light and wind upon the slopes. This is the area which exerted such a strong pull and influence on the life and music of Edward Elgar.

It was from his mother that Elgar inherited not only his deep and abiding love of poetry and literature but also his equal love and knowledge of the countryside. He knew many of the country crafts, and all his life walked and cycled the lanes of this area and knew them intimately. Elgar's susceptibility to the environment in which many of his works were created, or were influenced, is often indicated by either the titles of works or acknowledgements at the end of the score. Thus the piano piece *In Smyrna* is a momento of Elgar's Mediterranean cruise in 1905, and in particular his visit to a Turkish mosque; the *Scenes from the Bavarian Highlands* were the direct result of holidays in Bavaria from 1892 to 1895, while the concert overture *In the South (Alassio)* is a warm, sumptuously orchestrated tribute to his love for Italy. This country in particular seems to have been conducive to his inspiration. The Second Symphony bears the place-names Venice and Tintagel, while in the part-song *A Christmas Greeting,* written in Rome in 1907, Elgar and his wife, who wrote the poem, are dreaming nostalgically of far-away Herefordshire:

> On and on old Tiber speeds
> Dark with its weight of ancient crime:
> Far north, through green and quiet meads,
> Flows on the Wye midst mist and silvering rime.

One other area of England also played its part in the creation of some fine works. In 1918, Elgar, shocked by the horrors of war and weary of town life, had left London and was living in an isolated thatched cottage called 'Brinkwells', near Fittleworth, deep in the secluded woodlands of Sussex. It was here that he wrote his three great chamber works, the Violin Sonata, String Quartet and Piano Quintet, and also the Cello Concerto. We know that he was deeply affected by the peaceful woods of his surroundings, and also by a more sinister group of gnarled and twisted dead trees, whose influence can be felt very plainly in the Piano Quintet. However, all these works are shot through with an autumnal mellowness and wistfulness—it is music of woodland mists and mysteries.

Nonetheless, despite the influence of Italy and the Mediterranean, of Bavaria, of Sussex and London, it was the countryside into which he was born that had the most profound effect upon the man and his music.

*      *      *

# The composer and his environment

It is fascinating to speculate on the influence of landscape on the great composers. The music of certain composers has taken on the identity and characteristics of the landscape into which they were born so completely that the sound of one easily conjures up the visions of the other. The music of Sibelius, for instance, immediately brings to mind the bleak northern landscapes of his Finland. Composers often heightened the conscious nationality of their music by using indigenous folk-music. Thus the music of Grieg is associated with the mountains, forests and fjords of Norway, deliberately so when Grieg is using folk-tunes of Norway. When he does not use them his own characteristic styles of melody and harmony have also become redolent of that country's music-making. Similarly, the Englishness of the music of Vaughan Williams and Holst is based on their use of folk-music or the fact that their own original melodies often take on the flavour of English folk-music.

The danger inherent in this practice is that folk-music can tie a composer too much to the parish pump, so that his music becomes too national for international taste, and this has happened in the past with certain English composers. Fortunately the effect of the countryside is more often beneficial to composers than stifling. We know the joy both Haydn and Beethoven felt upon getting into the countryside—although Mozart, very much the townsman, was seemingly indifferent to it. A letter from his father on one of their tours speaks of driving in their carriage through miles of gorgeous countryside with Mozart never looking up once from his manuscript book.

Other composers have successfully captured the flavour of their country by using the dance rhythms of that country rather than actually quoting folk material; notable examples are Chopin, with his Polonaises and Mazurkas, and Liszt, with his Hungarian Rhapsodies. More interesting is the fact that without using any obvious nationalistic material a composer can still breathe into his music the very soul of his country. What makes Verdi's music so Italian? Why is Dvorak's music so redolent of Czechoslovakia? What speaks so clearly of Russia in the music of Tschaikowsky, Rimsky-Korsakov or Rachmaninoff?

Surely one reason is that from infancy all these men had in their blood and bones the feel of their country, the rhythmic and melodic characteristics and clichés, the natural and man-made sounds that give each country its own identity, and made it as natural for their music to speak this language as their own tongue.

The greatest English composer, Edward Elgar, also belongs in this category. His music is English, and yet not once in his music did he use a folk melody or nationalistic device of any sort. His music is English yet is firmly in the broad flow of European music that also encompasses the Germanic sounds of Wagner, the Italian Verdi, the Norwegian Grieg, and the Russian Rachmaninoff. Like those composers, Elgar was influenced by the landscape in which he lived, and certain areas of the country had an intense personal significance for him and his music. In particular, one such area has become so associated with the composer, and many of his major works, that it is not at all fanciful to call it 'Elgar Country'. It is the area in the triangle bounded by the three cathedral cities of Worcester, Hereford and Gloucester, with Malvern as a focal point. It was this area in which he was born, where he spent his happiest years, and where he returned to die. The names of the area, with two of its lovely rivers, the Severn and the Wye, run like *leit-motifs* throughout his life.

Once, during a discussion with her father, Elgar's daughter Carice asked why a genius should suddenly appear in a country or a particular family for no apparent reason. Elgar said that it was one of those mysterious things for which there is no accounting – it just was so. As to whether the country influences or makes the genius, Carice later wrote 'it is certain that no one was ever more involved with the very spirit and essence of his own country than E. It was in his very bones – Worcestershire was everything to him, the very look of spring coming, the cottages, the gardens, the fields and fruit orchards were different to his mind in Worcestershire from anywhere else. He loved England and would delight in seeing places new to him and get their atmosphere and understand the feeling of other parts of England – but Worcestershire remained supreme. From walking, driving and bicycling there was very little of the county he did not know, and his memory for every village however remote, and every lane however twisty and bewildering, was extraordinary. He had a wonderful gift of sense of locality and a wonderful memory.'

Many of the places closely associated with the composer still survive. The illustrations in this book try to recapture, as they are today, places Elgar knew well.

# The early struggle

Provincial, Victorian England, into which Elgar was born, was hardly the easiest place to begin a musical career. Since the death of Purcell in 1695, English music had been dominated by foreign musicians, particularly the Germans Handel and Mendelssohn, and although it had played host to many great composers since, notably Haydn, Chopin, Grieg, Saint-Saëns, Verdi and Dvorak, it was still slow to recognise native talent. Much of this was, in any case, completely dominated by the German influence, and such fine English musicians as Sullivan, Mackenzie, Parry and Stanford were unable to escape from it; their major symphonic works are strongly flavoured by Brahms. In addition, the stiff Victorian religiosity that coloured much choral music of that period was another suffocating influence. So the 'Das Land Ohne Musik' jibe was no joke, and such was the measure of Elgar's achievement that he not only placed English music on the international map after after 200 years but made it easier for the next generations of English composers to be taken seriously.

If being born into this background was not already a big enough handicap, Elgar had two other major obstacles loaded against him in class-conscious provincial England: he was the son of a tradesman and he was a Catholic.

Edward William Elgar was born on June 2nd 1857 in a small cottage at Broadheath, a village three miles from Worcester. The family left the cottage in 1859 and went to live in Worcester, at 1 Edgar Street (now demolished), then in 1861 they moved to 2 College Precincts, in the shadow of the Cathedral. They eventually settled, in 1863, in High Street, where William Henry Elgar, Edward's father, had a music shop. Worcester was then a small, quiet city, dominated by the cathedral on the banks of the River Severn. Unfortunately, progress in general and the motor car in particular have ravaged this once beautiful city, although there are still attractive corners to be found. The site of the Elgar music shop is now occupied by Russell and Dorrell's store, and it is marked by a plaque.

W H Elgar was the sort of practical musician indispensible to those small towns. As well as keeping the music shop, he tuned and repaired pianos, played violin in the local orchestra, sang in the glee clubs and was organist at the Catholic Church. The young Edward therefore had one advantage—that of growing up in a thoroughly practical musical atmosphere. He studied the sheet music and scores in the shop, read the theory books and musical tutors, and taught himself a variety of instruments: piano, organ, violin, cello, bassoon and trombone. And, apart from a dozen violin lessons in London, he remained a self-taught musician. Although Elgar may have regretted at the time his lack of opportunity to study at one of the musical colleges, with hindsight it is easy to see how much we owe to this fact. This lack of formal, and cramping, training forced his genius to take its natural course, and although the struggle to become a composer was long, hard and bitter, it nonetheless gave his style the personality and distinctiveness that it possesses.

When he left school, Elgar was put to study law, like Handel and Schumann before him. Also like them it was not long before he broke away to devote himself completely to music. He worked in his father's music shop; played second and, later, first violin in the local orchestra, and also in the Birmingham orchestra, and later succeeded his father at St George's Catholic Church as organist. He also taught the violin at Mount School, Malvern, but he hated teaching, likening it to 'turning a grindstone with a dislocated shoulder.' He also became musical director at Powick Lunatic Asylum, where the music he wrote for a varied collection of instruments proved an invaluable help to his understanding of orchestral resources.

This long period of apprenticeship gave Elgar a unique insight into the practicalities of instrumentation that never failed him in later life. He also became much in demand as a piano teacher. One of his pupils, Caroline Alice Roberts, he was later to marry, in 1889, much against the wishes of her aunts, who immediately cut her out of their wills for having the impertinence to marry the son of a tradesman, and one with seemingly few future prospects.

She was, after all, from a very different stratum of society. Her father was Major General Sir Henry Gee Roberts of the Indian Army, and she lived in a beautiful Georgian house with extensive views of the Malvern Hills, called Hazeldine House, in the village of Redmarley d'Abitot, just over the Gloucestershire border. She had published a two-volume novel and some poetry, had studied geology, took part in Shakespeare readings, sang in village concerts and in a choir which was often accompanied by a string orchestra in which Elgar played. Her family's fears were apparently borne out by the next few events—the Elgars moved to London to give Edward more chance of making a name for himself. Unfortunately the capital was not interested in provincial musicians; no-one wanted private lessons from him and no-one was interested in playing or publishing his music. In 1891, dispirited and exhausted, they moved back to Malvern to start the weary round of teaching and playing again.

# Elgar's birthplace

In 1856, when Elgar's parents moved to Broadheath, William Henry's piano-tuning business was flourishing. Particularly valuable to him were the contacts with the aristocratic families of the area, and he went regularly to tune the pianos at Witley Court (now an impressive ruin to the north-west of Worcester), Croome Court (south of Worcester, near Kempsey), and Madresfield Court (near Malvern). When on his visits he often used to take with him the young Edward, who was allowed to play in the grounds while his father went about his business. Later in life, when a famous composer, Edward was invited back to these great houses as an honoured guest of the families.

His mother's family, the Greenings, came from the villages of Elmore in Gloucestershire and Weston under Penyard in Herefordshire. They moved to Claines, north of Worcester, and it was while here that she first met William Henry Elgar, who came as a lodger. Anne was at this time employed at the Shades Tavern in Mealcheapen Street in Worcester (now much altered and at present a Calor Gas showroom). After their marriage they moved to rooms in College Precincts, Worcester, an attractive row of houses opposite the cathedral, and in 1856 moved to the cottage called 'The Firs' which was to become known simply as the Elgar Birthplace.

The small brick cottage stands in the village of Lower Broadheath, three miles from Worcester. To one side of the cottage stand the stables built by Elgar's father and uncle, and by the side of them the graves of Mina and Marco, the two dogs who were Elgar's inseparable companions in the last years of his life. The family left this cottage in 1859, and it must by then have been very cramped, with the Elgar parents and four children, of whom Edward was the youngest. Worcester Corporation bought the cottage in 1935 and it is now a museum dedicated to Elgar's memory. It houses many mementos and possessions of the composer, as well as manuscripts and photographs. Books, records and music are on sale there, and it has become a place of pilgrimage for music-lovers from all over the world.

# Formal education

Elgar started to attend a 'dame school' at 11 Britannia Square, Worcester, when he was seven, in 1864. The school was run by a Miss Walsh, and he also received piano lessons at this time from a Miss Tyler. He attended the school with his brothers and sisters, and according to an account Elgar once drew up to show the expenses of his education, he attended the school for the sum of £1 per quarter annum.

After this Elgar went for a short time to a Roman Catholic school at Spetchley, three miles from Worcester on the Stratford Road. This was maintained by the Lord of the Manor, Robert Berkley. Although the education he received here apparently made no great impression on him, he once told Ernest Newman that 'as a boy he used to gaze from the school windows in rapt wonder at the great trees swaying in the wind; and he pointed out to me a passage in *Gerontius* in which he had recorded in music his subconscious memories of them' (*Sunday Times,* 23 October 1955). Could this be the passage in Part II, 'the summer wind among the lofty pines'? In later years Elgar often returned to Spetchley House as a guest of the

*Spetchley School*

Berkleys. The school itself is a Victorian red-brick building in the form of an H. It was designed by Pugin and built in 1841. It has a gabled slate roof with an open bellcote.

His final school was Littleton House, near Worcester, which he attended from the ages of eleven to fifteen. The school had about 30 pupils under the direction of their teacher, Mr Francis Reeve, who, in a scripture lesson, sowed the seeds of what was to become *The Apostles* in Elgar's mind. Elgar was eventually to become head boy of the school, for his last nine months.

The building is now a private house and is a listed Queen Anne building. It lies off the Malvern Road at Lower Wick, still standing in its own pleasant grounds. One notable feature of the house today is that the interior wood-panelling of the hall comes from the timber of ships, including the *Mauretania*.

*Above: Littleton House.*

*Left: 11 Britannia Square.*

# Claines Church

Three miles to the north of Worcester stands Claines Church. It is in this peaceful spot that Elgar's grandparents were buried, and it was to this churchyard that the teenage Elgar would come on a summer's day to sit and study scores. The tree-shaded churchyard is still quiet and serene. Not far away lies Broadheath Common, another favourite haunt of the young Elgar, and the place where in all probability the *Wand of Youth* music was hatched.

At this time he had just acquired the scores of the Beethoven symphonies, and he was particularly excited by the 'Pastoral' and the rapid modulations in the *Minuetto* of the First Symphony. Mendelssohn's music to *A Midsummer Night's Dream* was also studied here. This was to start a life-time habit of study or the planning of works in the open air. Whether he was walking, cycling, fishing or kite-flying the ideas would come to him, and even though the process of writing down and scoring had to be done at the music desk, it was invariably in the open air that the ideas were conceived. The Ordnance Survey Map still survives on which Elgar jotted down the theme of the fifth *Pomp and Circumstance March*—the only paper to hand on which to capture an idea that had occurred to him as he was driving through Gloucester in 1930.

But sitting in Claines churchyard as a boy with his scores was when Elgar must have first been aware of the music of that countryside that he was to translate back into such magical sounds. Later he was to say 'There is music in the air, music all around us, the world is full of it and you simply take as much as you require!'

# St George's Church

St George's Catholic Church, in Sansome Place, Worcester, was built in 1829 on the site of an earlier chapel. The side-altars and stone facade, the high altar and the sanctuary were added in 1895. The picture over the high altar is a copy of Raphael's 'Transfiguration', but the canvas was not allowed to be reproduced in one piece and has been seamed across the bottom. The paintings making up the side-panels were added in 1880.

On May 26, 1880, the new chancel was opened by Bishop Ullathorne. Elgar's father played the organ and Edward led the orchestra. He had written, especially for the occasion, *Domine salvam fac, Salve regina* and *Tantum Ergo*.

W H Elgar became organist there in 1842 and held the position until 1883. Edward often deputized for him as a young man, finally

succeeding him in that position in November 1885. Many of his early anthems for choir and organ were written for, and first performed at, St George's; hearing his own works performed, however unprofessionally, must have given some encouragement to the aspiring young composer.

Elgar played the bassoon in a wind quintet on Sunday afternoons at this time, and the sermon-time was often spent writing music in readiness for the afternoon's session. Percy Young, in *Elgar O.M.,* recounts an amusing incident of this time:

> There was an occasion when on a moonlit night outside the Leicester's house Edward took out his bassoon to assemble it in the street. 'Hi!' said a voice, 'if you shoot that here it'll cost you five shillings.'

# The 'Three Choirs' cities

The three West Country cathedral cities of Worcester, Hereford and Gloucester still contain much charm and history within their boundaries, and much that Elgar would still know and recognise, despite the destructive forces of time and 'progress'.

Gloucester is the largest and most industrial city, and has the fewest Elgarian associations, although the glorious cathedral is in many ways the finest of the three. Hereford is the smallest, and still retains much of the flavour of an old market town. The fact that traffic has been diverted from its centre adds much to its charm. Hereford and its county were well loved by Elgar and he lived here for seven years. But inevitably it is Worcester that retains the greatest Elgarian spirit. Apart from the few years spent in Hereford and London, he chose to live in Worcestershire all his life. His birthplace and grave both lie a short distance from the city, and within the city itself are many places connected with the composer: St George's Roman Catholic Church and, just along from it, the

*Gloucester Cathedral*

*Hereford Cathedral*

corner building which contained the solicitor's office of Mr William Allen, 7 Sansome Place, where Elgar worked for about a year; the houses at 4 Field Terrace and 35 Chestnut Walk (Loretto Villa – now number 12), where he lived with his married sisters before his marriage; the flats, now called Elgar Court, where his last home stood; and, of course, the magnificent cathedral, which dominated the small city of Elgar's youth.

After the service at St George's finished on a Sunday morning the young Elgar would run to the cathedral so that he could catch the organ music at the end of the service there, and it was in this cathedral that so many of Elgar's masterpieces came to life under his baton. There is now a stained-glass window in his memory erected above the spot where Elgar used to stand to listen to performances of his oratorios, behind a pillar hidden from the congregation but where he could watch the orchestra.

In the High Street stands the fine Guildhall designed by a pupil of Sir Christopher Wren. It now contains the bronze bust of Elgar sculpted in 1935 by Donald Gilbert and the Burne Jones portrait of the composer. It was here that Elgar received the Freedom of the City of Worcester, and then walked in procession along the High Street to the cathedral, passing his father's old music shop. This end of High Street, nearest the cathedral, has been much altered since

Elgar's day, but lower down the facades of the buildings, if not the shops beneath them are still the same. At the end of High Street, facing the cathedral, stands the statue of Elgar, sculpted by Kenneth Potts, which was unveiled on June 2nd 1981 by HRH The Prince of Wales.

Not far away, in Broad Street, stands the Crown Hotel, home of the Worcester Glee Club, established in 1810. The club members met here to drink and smoke at long candlelit tables while music was performed. Elgar's father had been a member for many years and introduced Edward at the age of about twelve. He started by accompanying the singers, but later he was to become a violinist, composer, arranger, and eventually conductor in 1879. In February 1910, Elgar revisited the Glee Club and took the chair. He was described thus by someone present:

> Hair now very grey, but otherwise unchanged in appearances. Eyes open and shut rapidly and continuously, hands small, slender and nervous. Right hand shakes nervously as it rests on table. Complexion rather dark, almost olive colour, strong well-shaped moustache, nose almost hooked. Teeth large, strong, white and show when he smiles. Speaks rapidly, sharply and distinctly. Not very loud but clear.
>
> (Diana McVeagh: *Edward Elgar, his life and music*)

The room in which the Glee Club was held is now called the Elgar Suite. It is to the rear of the hotel on the first floor. The oval-shaped room has three panels at each side and three at each end. Between these are half-columns with Ionic capitals. During restoration work in 1979 it was possible to see the original design of the panels, which were black with unusual coloured linear motifs. This presumably was the decoration in Elgar's day. The room has beautiful intricate plaster mouldings and there is a central portion of the roof which is raised with windows set in. The acoustics are remarkably good.

Every year in rotation the cities play host to the Three Choirs Festival. This, the oldest music festival in Europe, began in the early 18th century when the three cathedral choirs came together to 'make musick'. The earliest recorded meeting was at Worcester in 1719 but as it was described as a 'yearly Musical Assembly' it is clear that this was not the first. By the late 19th century the pattern was established—the three cathedral choirs were joined by a large contingent of amateurs, the 'Festival Chorus', to perform not only the established choral works but newly-commissioned ones also.

It had become an important musical event to which any composer would have been grateful to submit a work for performance; not only eminent British composers but world figures of the stature of Dvorak (in 1884) and Saint-Saëns (in 1913) had premieres at the festival.

*Worcester Cathedral*

One of the differences in Elgar's day was that instead of using a professional orchestra, as now, the players were all recruited locally. In 1878, Elgar played for the first time among the second violins in the festival orchestra, and was promoted to the first violins in 1881. The music included, as well as established masterpieces by Handel, Bach, Haydn, Mendelssohn, Beethoven and Brahms, works now totally forgotten by English composers such as Mackenzie, Cowen, Caldicott, J F Barnett and Parry. It was perhaps the acceptance of these that made Elgar, as late as 1893, scribble dejectedly on his festival programme: 'I played 1st violin for the sake of the fee as I cd obtain no recognition as a composer. E.E.'

Over the years his gradual emergence to international fame changed that, and after the First World War no festival would have been complete without the presence of Elgar himself, or his works, which made up a considerable bulk of the programme. Yet surprisingly few of his works received their premiere at a Three Choirs meeting—those that did included his first large-scale orchestral work, the overture *Froissart* (Worcester, 1890); *The Light of Life* (Worcester, 1896); *Te Deum and Benedictus,* Op 34 (Hereford, 1897); The second *Wand of Youth Suite* (Worcester, 1908); the fine unaccompanied part-song *Go Song of Mine* (Hereford, 1909); and the orchestral version of the *Severn Suite* (Worcester, 1932).

In Elgar's day the festival was held in September, but has now moved to late August. To take part in this full week of music-making in these idyllic surroundings is a delight of the first order, and to hear Elgar's works, especially the great oratorios, in these cathedrals is to realise that here is a perfect unity of architecture and music: splendid though they sound in the concert hall, there is a special spiritual affinity between these works and these majestic buildings, in which they sound so right.

Neville Cardus, in his chapter on Elgar in *Ten Composers,* aptly writes:

> We know his secret who have listened to Elgar during the music festivals held in the cathedral cities of Worcester, Gloucester and Hereford at the time of ripening summer. Here at the harvest of the year, in country washed by the rivers of the west, we have known music as music everywhere should be; part of the soil, creative, free, serious, life-giving.

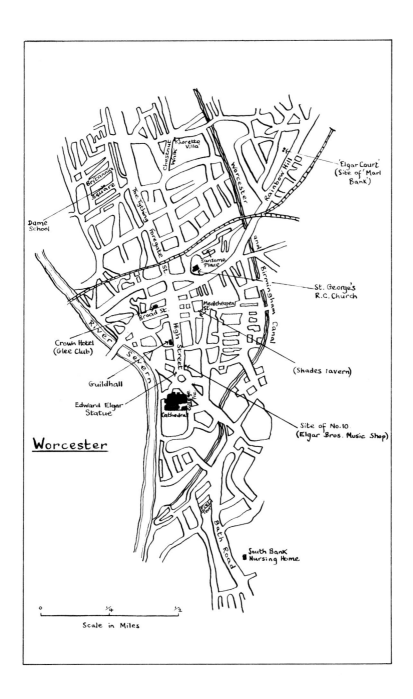

Worcester

'Elgar Court' (Site of 'Marl Bank')

Dame School

St. George's R.C. Church

Crown Hotel (Glee Club)

Guildhall

Edward Elgar Statue

(Shades Tavern)

Site of No.10 (Elgar Bros. Music Shop)

South Bank Nursing Home

Britannia Square

Chestnut Walk

Loretto Villa

The Tything

Foregate St.

Worcester

Rainbow Hill

Sansome Place

Mealcheapen St.

Broad St.

High Street

River Severn

and Birmingham Canal

Cathedral

Bath Road

0    1/4    1/2

Scale in Miles

# Malvern

The foundation of a Benedictine monastery in the 11th century probably started a settlement here, but its growth may have stemmed from the publication by Doctor Wall in 1756 of a treatise extolling medicinal virtues of the waters of the Malvern Wells. Thus the town grew and by the mid-19th century rivalled such resorts at Bath, Cheltenham and Buxton in popularity.

Great Malvern, Malvern Wells and Little Malvern are strung along the Worcester side of the Malvern Hills, while on the other side, but linked to them, is West Malvern. Today the town is still one of the most attractive in Britain, the way it is terraced on the slopes of the hills giving it a very Italianate flavour. It can have changed little since Elgar knew it: the wide streets with their large villas; the Abbey Gateway over the road next to the Priory and leading to the Abbey Hotel, and over which Troyte Griffith ('Troyte' of the *Enigma Variations*) had his studios; and above all the sweep of the Malvern Hills, its Pre-Cambrian rocks among the most ancient in the world.

The place still carries its air of a Victorian spa town, and with Worcester is still full of Elgarian associations. Here he had two of his homes, 'Forli' and 'Craeg Lea'; here in a rented room in the Cecilia Hall he gave his music lessons to the children of the wealthy – and there were many in Malvern; here he taught violin at the Mount School, an experience which did him and his pupils little good; and here he lies buried. It is not hard to imagine, too, the impact that the magnificence of the views from the Malvern Hills had on him.

Several of the houses where he was made welcome still exist. The Fittons were a musical family whose home 'Fairlea' still stands at the corner of Graham Road and Zetland Road. Elgar enjoyed music-making with the two Fitton girls, and Mrs Fitton, an excellent pianist, often entertained the Elgars. A piece for violin and piano, *Pastourelle,* was dedicated to Hilda; Isabel became the sixth variation in the *Enigma Variations,* and two part-songs, *The Snow* and *Fly, Singing Bird,* were dedicated to Mrs Fitton.

Close to Birchwood, to the west of Malvern, lies the magnificent 18th-century home of the Norbury sisters, Florence and Winifred (the latter was the eighth *Enigma* variation). 'Sherridge', more than Winifred, inspired this particular variation, for although it is headed 'W.N.', Elgar said that it was 'really suggested by an eighteenth-century house'. Winifred often made the short trip

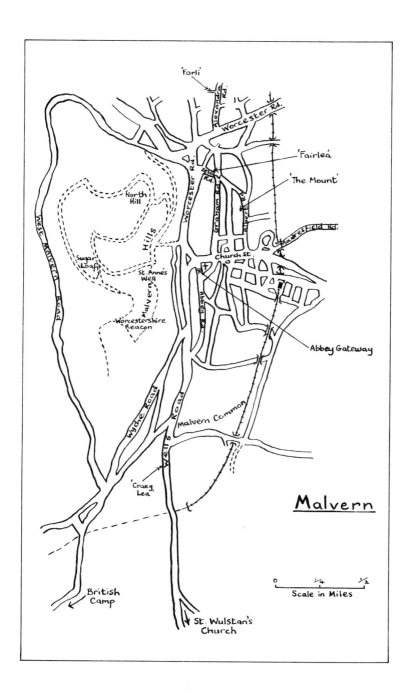

'Forli'

Alexandra Rd.

Worcester Rd.

'Fairleá

'The Mount'

North Hill

Hills

Worcester Rd.

Graham Rd.

Abbey Rd.

Hadresfield Rd.

Church St.

West Malvern Road

Sugar Loaf

St. Anne's Well

Malvern

Worcestershire Beacon

Priory Rd.

Abbey Gateway

Wyche Road

Wells Road

Malvern Common

'Craeg Lea'

Malvern

0    ¼    ½
Scale in Miles

British Camp

St. Wulstan's Church

through the woods to Birchwood to help with the copying of parts for *Caractacus*.

Elgar was also a regular guest at Hasfield Court, the home of William Meath Baker (the fourth variation), which lies between Malvern and Gloucester. The Elgars often visited Madresfield Court, near Malvern, the Tudor mansion of the Lygon family. Lady Mary Lygon was also commemorated in the *Enigma Variations*.

Not far from Malvern, on the Worcester road, stands the Powick Hospital, called in Elgar's day the County and City of Worcester Pauper Lunatic Asylum. From 1879 to 1884 Elgar was bandmaster here at a salary of £32 per annum, and for the regular series of concerts and dances wrote music, receiving five shillings for every polka and quadrille and one shilling and sixpence for accompaniments to the popular ditties of the day. Elgar had at his disposal a motley collection of instruments, but the material he wrote here, like much of his early sketches, not only taught him a lot about instrumental writing but yielded up many valuable ideas for later works.

Percy Young, in *Elgar O.M.*, tells us that 'In old age he liked to deflate affectation on the part of sycophantic visitors by commencing a conversation—"When I was at the Lunatic Asylum . . ."' Certainly few composers can have had such an unusual schooling in orchestration.

*Powick Asylum*

Madresfield Court

*Above: Malvern*

*Right: Sherridge*

*Above: High Street, Worcester, looking towards the Cathedral, in Elgar's day. The Elgar Music Shop is visible on the left.*

*Below: High Street, Worcester – facing the opposite direction.*

*Above: A favourite pastime – Elgar cycling in the Malvern countryside on his bicycle, 'Mr Phoebus'.*

*Below: Another favourite pastime – fishing.*

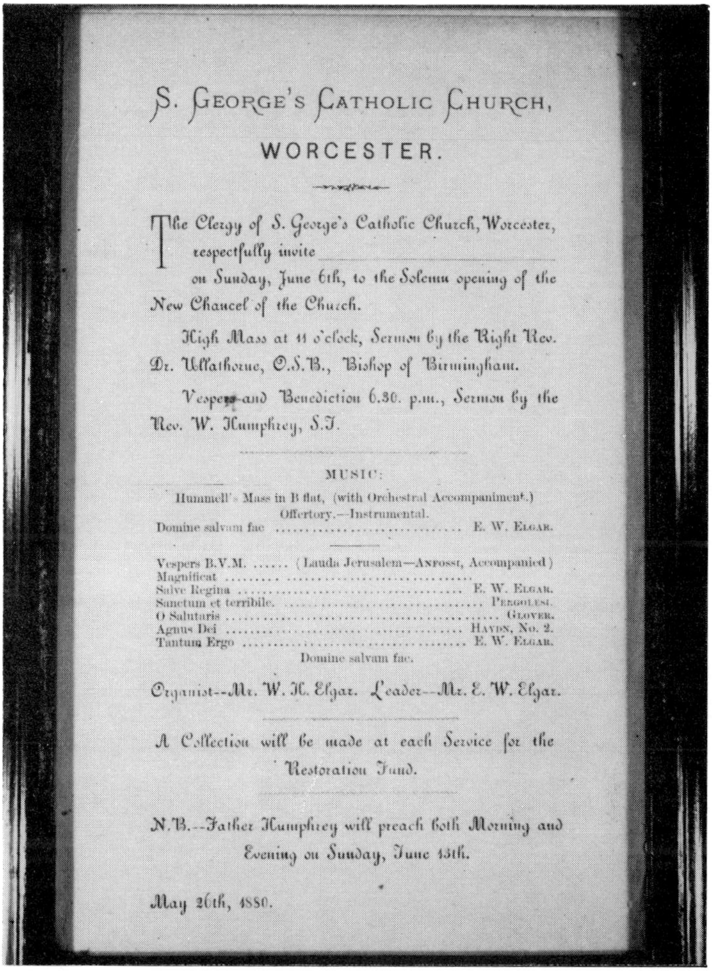

# S. GEORGE'S CATHOLIC CHURCH,
## WORCESTER.

The Clergy of S. George's Catholic Church, Worcester, respectfully invite _____

on Sunday, June 6th, to the Solemn opening of the New Chancel of the Church.

High Mass at 11 o'clock, Sermon by the Right Rev. Dr. Ullathorne, O.S.B., Bishop of Birmingham.

Vespers and Benediction 6.30. p.m., Sermon by the Rev. W. Humphrey, S.J.

---

MUSIC:

Hummell's Mass in B flat, (with Orchestral Accompaniment.)
Offertory.—Instrumental.
Domine salvam fac .............................. E. W. ELGAR.

---

Vespers B.V.M. ....... (Lauda Jerusalem—ANFOSSI, Accompanied)
Magnificat .....................................................
Salve Regina ...................................... E. W. ELGAR.
Sanctus et terribile............................... PERGOLESI.
O Salutaris ........................................... GLOVER.
Agnus Dei ...................................... HAYDN, No. 2.
Tantum Ergo ...................................... E. W. ELGAR.
Domine salvam fac.

Organist--Mr. W. H. Elgar.   Leader--Mr. E. W. Elgar.

A Collection will be made at each Service for the Restoration Fund.

N.B.--Father Humphrey will preach both Morning and Evening on Sunday, June 13th.

May 26th, 1880.

---

_Programme at St George's Church, Worcester, for May 26, 1880, to mark the opening of the new chancel. The organist was Elgar's father and Elgar was leader of the orchestra. Included in the music were Elgar's 'Domine salvam fac', 'Salve Regina' and 'Tantum Ergo'._

*Elgar at Gloucester in 1922.*

# 'Forli'

In June, 1891, after the unsuccessful foray to London, the Elgars moved to a stone-built house in Alexandra Road, Malvern, which they named 'Forli', after the early Italian painter of angel musicians. This was their home for the next eight years—years which saw Elgar's gradual rise from an obscure provincial musician to a composer of international rank. The works written at 'Forli' in these years include *The Black Knight; Serenade for Strings; Sursum Corda,* written for the Duke of York's visit to Worcester Cathedral in 1894; *Scenes from the Bavarian Highlands;* some charming part-songs, including *The Snow* and *Fly, Singing Bird;* the *Organ Sonata,* written for a convention of American organists at Worcester Cathedral in 1895; the *Imperial March;* and those two splendid cantatas, *King Olaf* and *Caractacus.* The performance, success and acceptance into the repertoire of these works had brought Elgar national fame.

One more work finished at 'Forli' set the seal on this triumph: the *Enigma Variations,* first conducted in 1899 by the great Hungarian conductor Hans Richter, showed England at last that she had

## IX.

### (Nimrod.)

produced a composer of the first rank. Richter, who had championed the music of Wagner, Brahms, Dvorak and Tschaikowsky, and had known the composers personally, now did the same for Elgar, recognising in him a greatness similar to that he had seen in the others.

'Forli' is still situated in a quiet walk off Alexander Road. In summer, creeper now obscures much of the attractive stonework. Opposite the house where Elgar had written the *Imperial March* in a bell-tent pitched on the grass, stands a new bungalow called 'Nimrod'.

# Herefordshire Beacon

The Hereford Beacon is one of the most dramatic summits of the Malvern range. Situated on the Herefordshire-Worcestershire border at 1114 ft. above sea level, it is the site of a remarkable Iron Age camp covering 44 acres. The intricate network of ditches and earthworks cut into the hillside must have made it a formidable stronghold to attack. Very early pottery has identified the Celtic people who first fortified the camp.

*(The Shell Guide to England)*

The landscape of Elgar's youth was now to play a major influence on an important work. In a letter dated December 11th, 1898, Elgar's mother wrote to her daughter Polly:

It has just occurred to me I never told you about 'Caractacus'—when I was at Colwall E(dward) and Alice came to see me—on going out we stood at the door looking along the back of the Hills—the Beacon was in full view—I said Oh! Ed., look at the lovely old Hill. Can't we write some tale about it. I quite long to have something worked up about it; so full of interest and so much historical interest . . . and in less than a month he told me 'Caractacus' was all cut and dried—and he had begun to work at it.

The story of the cantata concerns the defeat of the British tribes led by Caractacus as they take their last stand on these hills against

SCENE III.

THE FOREST NEAR THE SEVERN. MORNING.

the invading Roman forces. Thus, while the splendidly brazen 'Triumphal Procession into Rome' is a marvellous moment in the score, the most atmospheric passages are those linked with Elgar's own countryside—'British Camp on the Malvern Hills. Night' and especially 'The Forest Near the Severn. Morning.'

In January, 1934, as Elgar lay dying in his Worcester home, he was able to supervise by land-line a rehearsal in London of two excerpts from *Caractacus*. Afterwards he asked for the 'Woodland Interlude' to be repeated. It was no doubt this evocative music that reminded the old composer of his own boyhood and youth with so many happy hours spent beside the Severn.

# 'Craeg Lea'

In March 1899 the Elgars moved to a bigger house on the Wells Road, Malvern. Elgar named it 'Craeg Lea', an anagram of the names C A E Elgar (Alice, Edward and Carice, their daughter, whose name in turn derived from Caroline Alice). The house, looking today remarkably like it did when Elgar lived there, faces magnificent views across Worcestershire, while behind it the Malvern Hills rise steeply. An interview at this time quotes Elgar:

> A country life I find absolutely essential to me, and here the conditions are exactly what I require. As you see (and Dr. Elgar moved over to the large window which takes up the whole of one side of the study) I get a wonderful view of the surrounding country. I can see across Worcestershire, to Edgehill, the Cathedral of Worcester, the Abbeys of Pershore and Tewkesbury, and even the smoke from around Birmingham.

Walking the hills and cycling for miles along the lanes were his chief relaxations, and this idyllic peace and happiness, especially following the success of the *Enigma Variations,* released the floodgates of inspiration. England had at last produced a major composer and Elgar himself was conscious of this.

Masterpiece followed masterpiece: *Sea Pictures; The Dream of Gerontius,* whose disastrous first performance was later overcome by its success in Germany and with German musicians, particularly Richard Strauss; the *Cockaigne Overture;* the first two *Pomp and Circumstance Marches;* and the noble *Grania and Diarmid* music, especially the magnificent *Funeral March,* which brought forth the comment from W B Yeats that Elgar's music was 'wonderful in its heroic melancholy'—a phrase which aptly sums up so much of his music.

The last project of the 'Craeg Lea' days was the oratorio *The Apostles,* finished in 1903, and intended to be the first of a trilogy, although only *The Kingdom* was to follow; and a holiday in Alassio in Italy brought forth the overture *In the South,* first performed at an all-Elgar festival at Covent Garden in March 1904.

The great composer was now a public figure. Demands on his time as a conductor were increasing, particularly in London, but instead of turning to the metropolis as the centre of musical life, the family moved again to a bigger house, this time in Hereford. The public figure was not going to dominate the real, country-loving Elgar.

# Longdon Marsh

Some seven miles south-east of Malvern lies the small village of Longdon. The score of *The Apostles* bears the inscription 'In Longdon Marsh 1902-3'. Elgar would cycle from 'Craeg Lea' to spend the day here in the utter stillness and peace of this stretch of countryside to think out the grand design of this work. Longdon Marsh is a large area of flat meadows interlaced by row upon row of Pollard Willows. In the distance the Malvern Hills can be discerned. In the darkening evenings this almost desolate area has an eerie, haunted quality:

> Here he used to sit and dream. A great deal of *The Apostles* took shape in his mind there. He told me . . . he had to go there more than once to think out those climaxes in the Ascension . . .
> (W H Reed, *Elgar as I knew him*)

Once against the Worcestershire countryside had helped to shape the inspiration of a great work.

Two miles further on, nestling in a clump of trees, is the isolated Queenhill church. The porch was another favourite haunt of Elgar's when he was working on *The Apostles*. It is a Victorian addition which leads to a Norman doorway and a massive studded oak door. A motorway now cuts a channel not far from the church, but when sitting in the porch even this is mercifully invisible and does not dispel the serenity of the surroundings.

# THE APOSTLES.

## PROLOGUE.

Edward Elgar, Op.49.

11645

B

*Queenhill Church*

*Malvern Hills*

# 'Birchwood Lodge'

Of all the houses in which Elgar lived and worked, 'Birchwood Lodge' seemed the closest to his heart. He rented it as a summer retreat from 1898 to 1903, and would have bought it if the lease had been available. It is still remote, reached only by narrow, twisting lanes near the tiny village of Storridge, on the west side of the Malvern Hills. In Elgar's day the cottage must have been even more inaccessible when bicycle or pony trap were the only means of reaching it. Contemporary photographs show it to be surrounded by woods. Today the trees have been cleared from around the cottage, two annexes have been added, and the exterior has been painted. However, from all around are the same magnificent views. Elgar's study, at the front on the first floor, overlooked the range of

*Woods near Birchwood*

the Malvern Hills with the distant Beacon. As well as the seclusion of the cottage it was the surrounding woodlands which enchanted him. 'The trees are singing my music—or have I sung theirs? I suppose I have? It's too lovely here,' he wrote to Jaeger ('Nimrod' of the *Enigma Variations*) in 1900.

Dora Powell ('Dorabella' of the *Enigma Variations*) mentions in her book *Edward Elgar, Memories of a Variation* her visit to Birchwood, and the music of *Gerontius* being composed and played in those beautiful surroundings:

> I had bicycled from Wolverhampton, forty miles, and arrived, rather warm and dusty, at the cart-track leading up through the woods to the house. When I was nearly there I thought I would rest, out of sight, and yet cool. I heard the piano in the distance and, not wishing to lose more of it than I need, I soon went on. In a moment I came in sight of the Lady sitting on a fallen tree just below the windows. She had a red parasol. I think she sat there partly to warn people off—particularly people with bicycles who had been known to commit the awful crime of ringing a bell to announce their arrival. Leaning the bicycle against a tree, I went and sat down by her without speaking. He was playing the opening of Part II, and those who know the music will understand what it was like to hear that strangely aloof, ethereal music for the first time in such surroundings. Each time I hear it I think of that beautiful place and that glorious day with the sunshine coming through the lace-work of greenery and branches and the deep blue sky over all.

His letters to Jaeger, always a good indication of the state of mind at any one time, are always full of joy and happiness when written from 'Birchwood'. The relief he obviously felt at getting there is mirrored closely in his letters. 'Birchwood Lodge (Deo Gratias)' is the heading of many of his letters, and his love of the place is always evident:

> I say I wish you were here! I've been cutting a long path thro' the dense jungle like primitive man only with more clothes. But you will see our 'woodlands' some day. I made old Caractacus stop as if broken down on p.168 and choke and say 'woodlands' again because I am so madly devoted to my woods. I've got the place for years now and another summer—ja! (August 21 1898).

> Birchwood Lodge, near Malvern. Saturday, date and month and year unknown 'cos it's Birchwood. (probably November 1898)

> Well: here we are! There are a lot of young hawks flying about—plovers also—150 rabbits under the window and the blackbirds eating cherries like mad. E.E. is cheerful and is now learning potato culture. (July 5 1900)

> I hope you're better the heat has been really awful and upsetting everyone—I don't like to say a word about these woods for fear you shd. feel envious but it is godlike in the shade with the snakes and other cool creatures walking about as I write my miserable music. Is it music. I fear not. (August 1900).

> One line to catch post: I was out all day yesterday with a sawmill, sawing timber into joists, planks, posts, rafters, boarding yea! boarding with a feather edge: how little ye townsmen know of real life. (August 1900)

> Now, please address Craeglea after Tuesday next: we climb down to the valley on Wedy. am. and I cuss every step away from these woods. Grrrhh! (August 1900)

The solitude so essential to him was soon to disappear. The fact that he was not able to buy 'Birchwood' was a bigger blow to him that he admitted to his family. In a letter of August 27th 1903, Elgar wrote to Jaeger again:

> You saw my dear place and I hate having to give it up. My life is one continual giving up of little things which I love, and only great ones, I'm told, come into it, and I loathe them.

Michael Kennedy, in *Portrait of Elgar,* writes:

> But Arnold Bax, who had first met him there, sensitively perceived what the cottage meant to Elgar. In 1910 Bax was invited to submit a work for a Promenade Concert and Wood told him it was Elgar who had recommended Bax's work—'It seems that he never forgot my visit to Birchwood (I think his days there counted as the happiest in his tormented life, and he kept a special regard for anyone who had seen him in those surroundings).'

Although Elgar worked on *Caractacus* and *Sea Pictures* at Birchwood, its greatest memorial is *The Dream of Gerontius*. At the end of the score is written 'Birchwood. In summer. 1900'. Those magical, mystical sounds, written at white heat in those idyllic surroundings, still burn with the fervent passion of that inner vision so clearly encouraged by this spot.

*'The Dream of Gerontius': opening of Part 2.*

# 'Plâs Gwyn'

On 1st July 1904 the Elgars moved into 'Plâs Gwyn' in Vineyard Road on the edge of Hereford. One of Edward's diversions at this time was fishing:

> The advantage of this expensively rented property was its proximity to the Wye. Mordiford village was near at hand—ten minutes by bicycle— and Elgar spent many summer hours thereabout in the next few years.
>
> (Percy Young, *Elgar O.M.*)

One of the first visitors to this spacious property was 'Dorabella'. Alice enthused to her: 'I think great music can be written here, dear Dora, don't you?' Four days after their removal to Hereford, Elgar went to Buckingham Palace to receive his knighthood, and the following year he received the Freedom of the City of Worcester. That same year he accepted a post specially created for him, the professorship of music in the new University of Birmingham, a post which he occupied unhappily for three years until with relief he was able to resign.

But the private Elgar continued as before, fishing, cycling, walking, and a new hobby—chemistry. He converted an outhouse of 'Plâs Gwyn' into a laboratory, called it 'The Ark', and amidst explosions and other setbacks, actually patented a process for making sulphuretted hydrogen, and invented a kind of soap. The stories of his chemical disasters became as legion as those concerning his breathtaking ability for backing the wrong horse at the races were to become later in life.

Great music *was* written at 'Plâs Gwyn', however. One of the first of the major works to appear was the *Introduction and Allegro* for strings, based on an idea first heard in some distant singing on a Welsh holiday, and later again in the Wye Valley. Elgar said the work was a tribute to 'that sweet borderland where I have made my home.'

*The Kingdom* followed in 1906; the *First Symphony* in 1908; the *Violin Concerto* and *Bassoon Romance* in 1910; and the *Second Symphony* in 1911. The last-named work bears the inscription 'Venice-Tintagel' to emphasise the importance of the inspiration of those recently visited places, but much of the work was completed at 'Plâs Gwyn'.

In the Coronation Honours of 1911 Elgar was awarded the Order of Merit. The flow of masterpieces, and the OM, finally decided Lady Elgar that they must move to London, and the increasing necessity for Elgar's presence there seemed to make the

move inevitable. In 1910 the Elgars had taken a flat in London to try the idea of living there, but it was not to Sir Edward's taste. 'There is really no place for me here' he wrote to Alice Stuart-Wortley. Nonetheless, at the beginning of 1912 they moved into a large house in Hampstead which Elgar nostalgically called 'Severn House'. When 'Dorabella' came to see them and said that they must be in clover here, Elgar grumbled 'I don't know about the clover—I've left that behind at Hereford.'

# Mordiford Bridge

Ten minutes on a bicycle from 'Plãs Gwyn' lies the small village of Mordiford:

> The River Lugg starts in bleak moorland to the north of Radnor Forest . . . the Lugg runs into the Wye at Mordiford, having just been joined by the Frome on its way from the border town of Bromyard. It is one of the best streams in the country for grayling.
>
> Mordiford Bridge is one of the finest in the whole valley, its oldest parts dating from the fourteenth century.
>
> (H L V Fletcher: *Portrait of the Wye Valley*)

> In 1931, when the County Surveyor for Herefordshire, preparing a paper on 'The Art of the Bridge Builder'—for the Royal Society of Arts—wrote to him about his reputed connections with Mordiford Bridge, Elgar replied, saying, '. . . most of my "sketches", that is to say the original thoughts reduced to writing, have been made in the open air. I fished the Wye round about Mordiford and completed many pencil memoranda of compositions on the old bridge of which I hold many affectionate memories'.
>
> (Percy Young: *Elgar O.M.*)

The work most closely associated with Mordiford Bridge is *The Music Makers,* which, although finished in London in 1912, was sketched some years earlier, especially around Mordiford. Written on the sketches of the original score is the note 'Mem: four trout (decent) three (small) put back. Mr. D. hooked a salmon and lost it. Mordiford.'

Not far from Mordiford are the riverside villages of Holme Lacy and Hampton Bishop, where Elgar used to seek the peace and tranquillity necessary for his inspiration, and in whose meadows by the Wye he would practise throwing his boomerang with W H Reed. Also nearby was Belmont Abbey, which Elgar often attended, the calm, contemplative atmosphere being much to his liking.

*Final page of 'The Music Makers'*

# London and Sussex

Elgar lived in London from 1912 to 1923, the only period he spent away from his beloved West Country, apart from the two-year stay there immediately after his marriage. He was without doubt by now one of the world's most highly regarded composers. Every Elgar premiere was an event; and the world's greatest musicians took up and performed his music. He was the musical laureate of the age. The First World War soured this story, as it did so much else, and virtually swept away the England that Elgar knew and loved.

Many of Elgar's champions had been foreign, especially Germans, and the war affected him in a deeply personal way. Before this happened, however, the great works continued; *The Music Makers* was finished; the *Crown of India* was assembled with the help of ideas from his old sketch-books; his ballet *The Sanguine Fan*; the charming music to the play *The Starlight Express*; and the war works *Carillon, Le Drapeau Belge, Polonia* and the noble choral work *The Spirit of England.* Probably the greatest work to emerge from Severn House was *Falstaff,* the masterly symphonic study of Shakespeare's fat knight. Surely it is no accident that the most evocative and moving parts of the score are the 'Dream Interludes', when we are taken once again into deepest rural England, and the scene in Shallow's orchard in Gloucestershire.

From 1917 to 1921 Elgar finally escaped London to the cottage *near* called 'Brinkwells', deep in the Sussex countryside. The Elgars took *Fittleworth* this place as a summer retreat, and the *Cello Concerto* and chamber music was the direct result. Gone, however, was the old swagger and opulence of the music. A new, mellower, more austere Elgar was addressing his audience.

Suddenly, in 1920, Lady Elgar died. She had not only been his constant companion but his greatest inspiration and encouragement, especially in the early days, when it would have been all too easy to give up. Elgar knew this better than most: 'All I have done was owing to her and I am at present a sad and broken man—just stunned,' he wrote to Walford Davies.

'Severn House' was sold and for two years Elgar lived in the anonymity of a London flat and his clubs. Worcestershire called, however, and in 1923 he found a house in the village of Kempsey, five miles south of Worcester, and moved in that April.

# Napleton Grange

'Napleton Grange' is situated in a secluded lane in the small village of Kempsey. It is a fine, spacious, black-and-white timbered house looking as immaculate as it did then. The grounds are quite extensive and proved ideal for his newly acquired dogs that were now to provide him with such companionship. His creative spark, however, had died, and despite the urging of his friends nothing of substance came from his pen. He still had many conducting engagements, and there was the annual Three Choirs Festival, at which he was now the major figure. But as W H Reed, a close friend and leader of the London Symphony Orchestra, wrote: 'On returning to Kempsey he settled down again to the life of a country gentleman, reading a great deal, studying, and pursuing various hobbies.'

The only music dated from those years is the two sets of incidental music, for Binyon's *King Arthur* and the British Empire Exhibition at Wembley in 1924, and a few unaccompanied part-songs.

In 1927 the lease to 'Napleton Grange' expired and Elgar moved to 'Battenhall Manor', Worcester (said to be haunted), and then to 'Tiddington House', Stratford. Both these houses are now demolished, although a mulberry tree and a plaque in Arundel Drive commemorate the spot in the Battenhall Manor gardens where Elgar planted the tree. Of Tiddington House only the long wall that bordered the garden remains. In 1929 he made his final move. For the Worcester festival of that year he rented a large house on Rainbow Hill, Worcester, called 'Marl Bank'. He liked it there and later bought it, moving in December of that year.

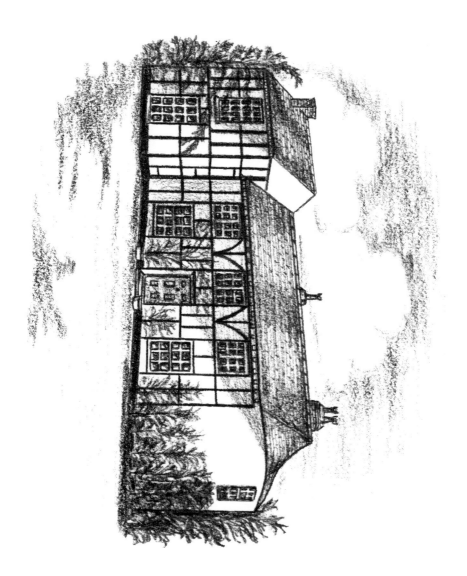

# 'Marl Bank'

Tragically, this fine house was demolished in 1969 to make room for flats, but it is still easy to see why the site appealed to Elgar. It overlooks the city he loved, with the cathedral rising majestically above the rooftops, and he could see in the distance the route he took to school as a boy 60 years before.

Here he continued to live the life of a country gentleman—the great composer in retirement. He developed an interest in horse racing, he tended his roses, and the gramophone provided a new distraction. He was the first great composer to record for posterity many of his major works, and he was as fascinated by the mechanical as by the musical side of it.

Anything associated with his childhood or past events he revisited and remembered. He liked to drive to the cottage at Broadheath where he was born; to Birchwood and Mordiford; he wrote a moving foreword to a book, *Forgotten Worcester,* by his childhood friend Hubert Leicester. When they widened the old familiar bridge across the Severn that he had known all his life, he bought a section of it and had it mounted in his garden at 'Marl Bank'; he could not bear to think of the old iron balustrades going for scrap.

Creatively, the old flame had started to burn again. His beloved river was featured for a final time in the *Severn Suite* of 1930,

written for the Crystal Palace Brass Band Festival and two years later rescored for orchestra. It is dedicated to a great friend and champion of Elgar's last years, George Bernard Shaw. In 1931 came the *Nursery Suite,* another nostalgic, backward-looking work, with its final violin cadenzas musing over the work's previous themes. The violin was Elgar's favourite instrument and this final cadenza seems a last regretful farewell to the instrument that had embodied so much of his secret hopes and aspirations as a young man. The first movement of the *Nursery Suite* quotes a hymn-tune that Elgar had written in 1878, 53 years earlier, and called 'Drakes Broughton'. This is the name of a village near Pershore, the exact significance of which to Elgar is now unclear. Basil Maine, in his book *Elgar: His Life and Works'* written in 1933, says:

> In any of the western festival cities Elgar can count on meeting people who have known him since his earliest appearances as a composer, and a few perhaps who have followed his progress since boyhood. It is but natural, therefore, that he is never happier than when he is in this part of the country, at his home on Rainbow Hill, or on a visit to Hereford or Gloucester. He knows every mile of that pleasant land. Along many of the roads he could walk, sleeping, and not lose the way. And in fancy he likes to think of himself in the years beyond life itself, moving leisurely along those green ways, perchance to surprise an old friend there who had accustomed himself to think of him as being eternally absent. There is one road in particular to which he intends to return, a secluded stretch of about a quarter of a mile which even at Summer's noon is darkened by tall trees, so that its shadow and its silence are one in their depth. It is not far from Drakes Broughton.

Other smaller works also appeared, but the two major works that he worked at with enthusiasm at the end of his life—the *Third Symphony* and the opera *The Spanish Lady*—remained unfinished and fragmentary at his death. Although the fifth *Pomp and Circumstance March* of 1930 recaptures the old flair and orchestral virtuosity, these last works have an appropriate autumnal mellowness and wistfulness about them.

After the Hereford Festival of 1933 he went to the Worcester South Bank Nursing Home. While here his thoughts still dwelt on his beloved rivers. He dictated a letter to Florence Norbury:

> I lie here hour after hour thinking of our beloved Teme—surely the most beautiful river that ever was and it belongs to you too—I love it more than any other—some day we will have a day together there—on it? by it? You shall choose the place . . .

Elgar had even wanted to be buried in the meadows below Powick where the Teme joins the Severn, but it was not to be. An operation revealed a malignant tumour. The end was near, and he was eventually moved back to 'Marl Bank'. The gramophone and the pleasure of supervising the *Caractacus* excerpts brightened his last days, but he died on February 23rd, 1934.

# St Wulstan's Church

After his wife's death in 1920 he wrote to his old friend Frank Schuster after the funeral: 'The place she chose long years ago is too sweet—the blossoms are white all round and the illimitable plain, with all the hills and churches in the distance which were hers from childhood, looks just the same—inscrutable and unchanging'. The burial was at St Wulstan's Roman Catholic Church, Little Malvern, just along the road from the old house 'Craeg Lea', and the gravestone was designed by their old friend from 'Enigma' days—Troyte Griffith. Now, 14 years later, Elgar was laid to rest in the same spot:

The funeral service, brief and simple, took place on the morning of Monday, February 26th. Snow scudded over the hills at the time, but soon there was brilliant sunshine. A handful of the closest friends, including the oldest of them all—Hubert Leicester, was all that attended. They wore no mourning. There were no flowers.

(Percy Young: *Elgar O.M.*)

The guide to the church records the memories of Mr Charles King, a parishioner, who recalled that the thing that stood out most clearly in his memory was how strongly and beautifully the birds were singing—almost as if they wished to pay their final tribute to the famous composer.

Standing today by the graveside the view is much the same. The Malvern Hills rise steeply over the road from the church, with the road itself later crossing between the peaks into Herefordshire. In the opposite direction the countryside drops away quickly to the vale of the River Severn. Below one can see the road winding into the distance, leading eventually to such favourite spots as Longdon and Kempsey. A tablet commemorating Elgar is now in Westminster Abbey, but one feels that here in Malvern is where his spirit hovers, and where his mortal remains should lie.

# Postscript

The outward image Elgar presented to the world, particularly in his last years, was that of a rather military-looking country squire who generally rebuffed any attempted talk about music. This mask—for such it was—covered a complex, sensitive, many-sided personality, and the many sides can be seen in the music. There is the ebullience and vigour of the *Pomp and Circumstance Marches,* the intense mysticism of the oratorios, the many noble and passionate passages in the symphonies, the delightful gaiety and wit of the *Wand of Youth* suites, and the out-of-doors exhilaration of the *Introduction and Allegro.* But often the anguish and the melancholy show through. Listen to *Sospiri* (Op.70), the *Cello Concerto,* or the private musings of the *Violin Concerto,* and one can sense the real inward Elgar. Or there is the 'heroic melancholy' of the slow movement of the *Second Symphony,* or 'Nimrod' of the *Enigma Variations.* J B Priestley, in his book *The Edwardians,* writes:

> It is the kind of passage, for ever recurring, when strings are quietened and the jagged thunder of his brass has gone, and like a purple-and-sepia sunset suddenly revealing patches of purest cerulean or fading apple-green, it is all different, strangely beautiful as music and catching at the heart because the man himself, no longer masterful, seems to be staring at us out of a sorrowful bewilderment. These moments when the persona is dropped are to me the secret of Elgar's lasting enchantment.

After his death the inevitable reaction set in, and succeeding generations saw only this persona, the mask, and accused his music of smugness and complacency. Astonishing though this seems to us today, one has only to remember that the generations following Haydn and Mozart saw only the powdered wigs and lace cuffs, and missed the passion underneath. Today, as in Elgar's day, leading international conductors perform and record his music, and with much of his major work now available on recordings, some of the more obscure pieces are being performed and recorded, and are found to be good.

For Elgar was incapable of writing a half-hearted note. Everything he did he meant, and his personal style and tone of voice is unmistakable. The long and bitter struggle he waged for recognition (did any other great composer take root from such unpromising soil?) left a scar on an already nervous and highly-strung disposition, and the facade that he adopted was a shield to cover this. Yet this struggle was the making of him. Without it his music could have ended up like the vast majority of other English composers' music of that generation—correct, well-mannered, gentlemanly and totally unmemorable. His music lives, it pulses with life. 'If you cut that it would bleed' was a favourite expression of his regarding his music.

But the earthly inner contentment of those rare beings that 'see visions and dream dreams' is not always cloudless. Sadly, despite his knighthood, his OM, being Master of the King's Musick, his numerous other decorations, honours, and doctorates, despite receiving honours from America and almost every European country, and despite the protestations of devoted friends, he went to his grave feeling that his music was misunderstood and would not last. His old world had been swept away by the war, and the cold wind of the 1920s blew much indifference across his reputation. However, Bach had to wait almost a hundred years for recognition, and, although Elgar's major works never really went out of fashion, the tremendous upsurge in interest in him and his music began only 30 years after his death (partly helped by Ken Russell's sympathetic film portrait for television) and has continued to gain momentum ever since. Elgar now belongs to the world as surely as does Bach, and yet in this corner of West Country England his spirit is still at its strongest.

An excerpt from the C Day-Lewis poem *Edward Elgar* recaptures this:

> For me, beyond the marches of his pride,
> Through the dark airs and rose-imperial themes,
> A far West-Country summer glares and glooms,
> A boy calls from the reeds on Severn side.
>
> And in it, too, in his music, I hear the famous river—
> Always and never the same, carrying far
> Beyond our view, reach after noble reach—
> That bears its sons away.

The Severn runs like a theme throughout his life: 'I am at heart the child on Severn side'. As a boy he was found on the river bank 'trying to write down what the reeds were saying.' When rehearsing the London Symphony Orchestra in his *First Symphony* he asked them to play the trio section of the second movement—an airy, dancing passage with flutes, solo violin and harps prominent—'like something you hear down by the river.'

> By some alchemy he put this into his music, a fresh, wistful quality, whenever his thoughts went back to his youth, to the land of lost content, alone by the river.

(Michael Kennedy: *Portrait of Elgar.*)

It is impossible , when standing in the meadows and lanes of Worcestershire and Herefordshire, or on the Malvern Hills, not to feel Elgar's music 'in the air, all around us.'

# Suggestions for further reading

There is a large bibliography. The most detailed works on his complex personality and life are *Elgar O.M.* by Percy Young, (White Lion Publications), *Portrait of Elgar* by Michael Kennedy (OUP) and Jerrold Northrop Moore's *Edward Elgar, A Creative Life* (OUP). Smaller works for more general reading are *Elgar* by Ian Parrott (Master Musicians Series, Dent), *Elgar* by Michael Hurd (Faber), *Elgar: His Life and Times* by Simon Mundy (Midas Books) and *Spirit of England* by Jerrold Northrop Moore (Heinemann). Many detailed and personal recollections are to be found in *Elgar: The Man and his Music* by Basil Maine (1933, reprinted by Chivers 1973), *Memories of a Variation* by Dora Powell (OUP, 1947), *Elgar as I knew him* by W H Reed (1936, reprinted Gollancz 1973), *Edward Elgar, The Record of a Friendship* by Rosa Burley and Frank Carruthers (Barrie and Jenkins), *The Elgar – Atkins Friendship* by E Wulston Atkins (David & Charles) and *An Elgar Companion* (ed. Christopher Redwood – Sequoia Publishing). For more detailed information on all Elgar's homes, with plans, illustrations and photographs, see *Elgar lived here* by Pauline Collett (Thames). The same author's *An Elgar Travelogue* (Thames) details Elgar's travels at home and abroad and the music that resulted from them. Quite indispensible is Jerrold Northrop Moore's book *Elgar: A Life in Photographs* (OUP), a photographic record of the composer's life. Finally, two collections of Elgar's letters also give a deep insight into his character: *Letters to Nimrod*, edited by Percy Young (Dobson), and *Letters of Edward Elgar* (Bles).

# Index

## to works by Elgar